David Lanz

sacred road

contents

HAL•LEONARD® CORPORATION

7777 W. BLUEMOUND RD. P.O. BOX 13819 MILWAUKEE, WI 53213

ISBN 0-7935-6896-X

Cover photo by Jim Goldsmith
Artist portrait by Rob v. Uchelen

Dreamer's Waltz

by David Lanz

A Path with Heart

by David Lanz

Take the High Road

by David Lanz

Brightly

14

Where the Tall Tree Grows

by David Lanz

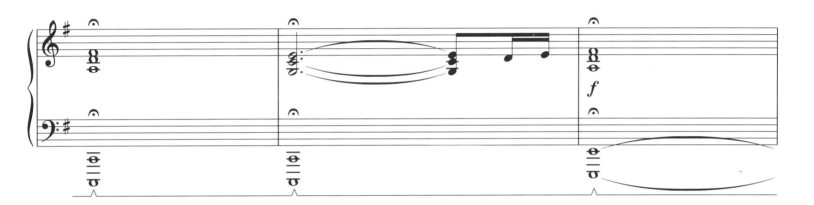

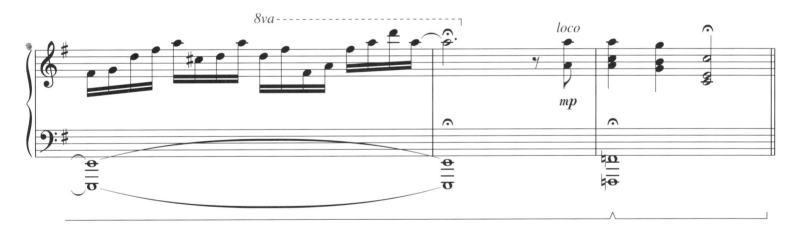

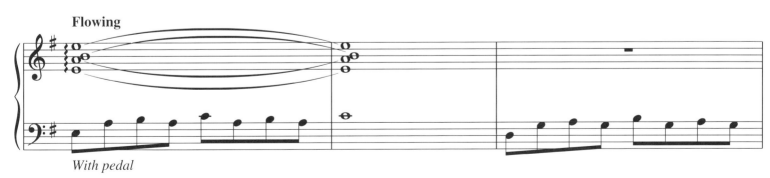

R.H.

Still Life

by David Lanz

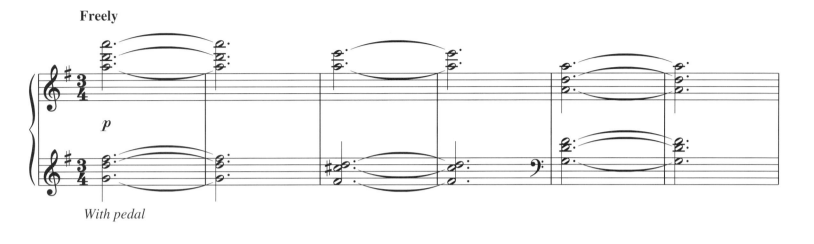

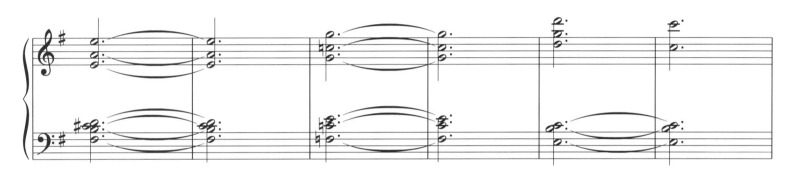

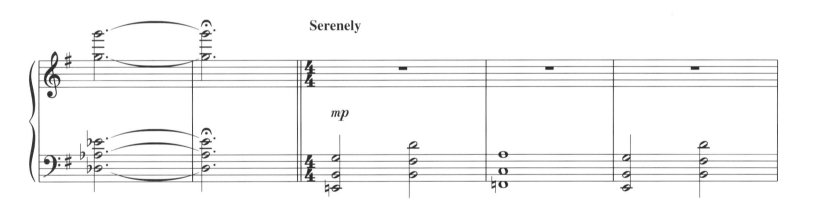

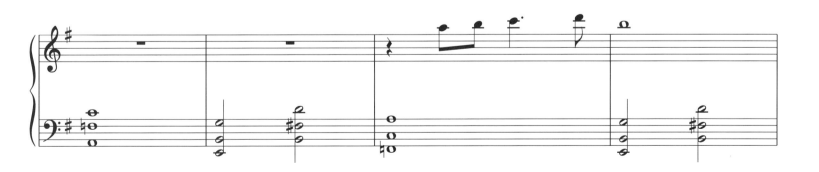

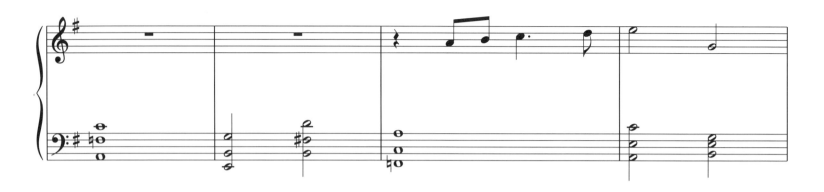

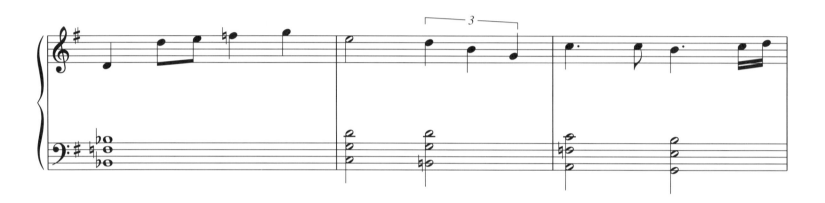

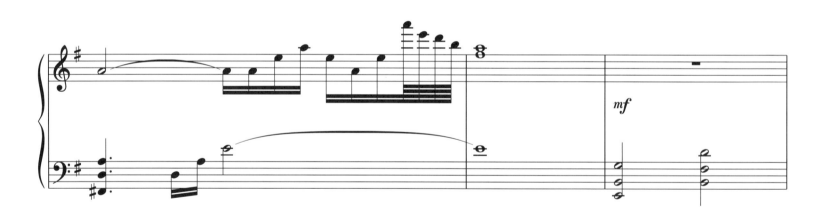

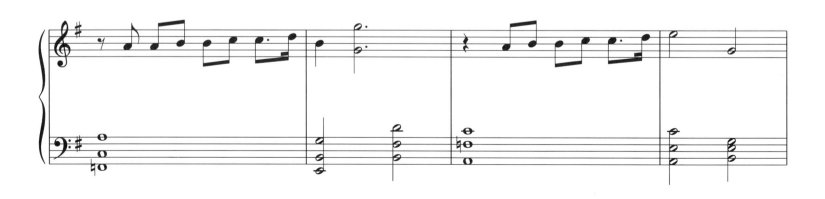

Brother Quixote

by David Lanz

Moderately

With pedal

The Long Goodbye

by David Lanz

Nocturne

by David Lanz

With feeling

Compassionata

by David Lanz

Slowly, reflectively

On Our Way Home

by David Lanz

Circle of Friends

by David Lanz

Before the Last Leaf Falls

by David Lanz

Sacred Road

by David Lanz

Peacefully

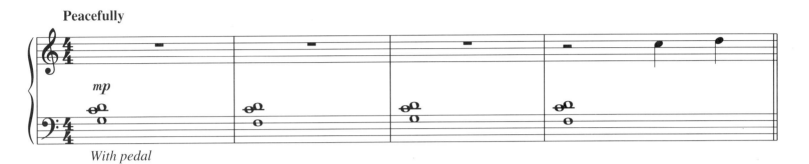

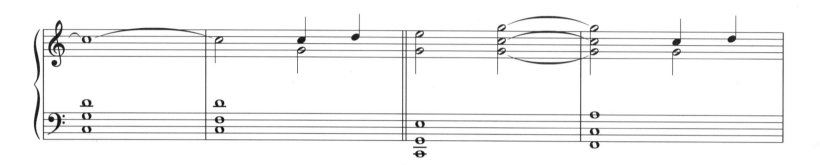

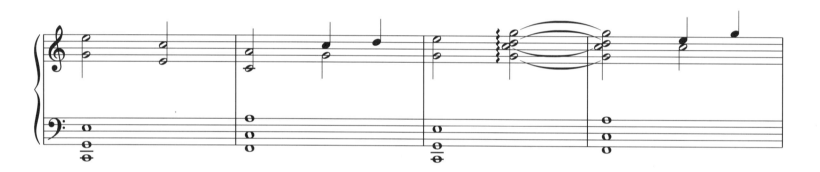

loco

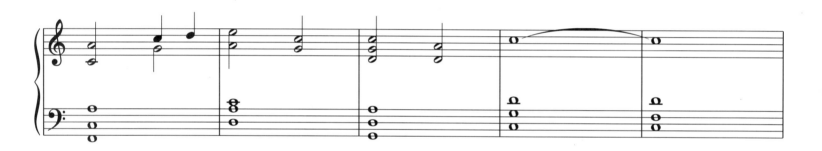

rit.

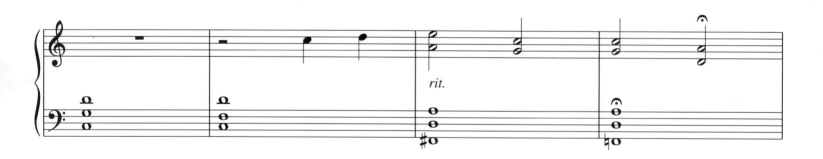

slowly

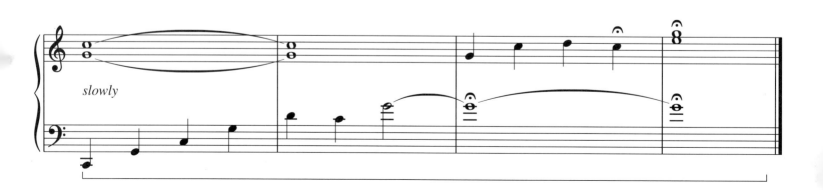

Beloved

by David Lanz

Gently

mp

With pedal

Variations on a Theme from Pachelbel's Canon in D Major

Arranged by
David Lanz

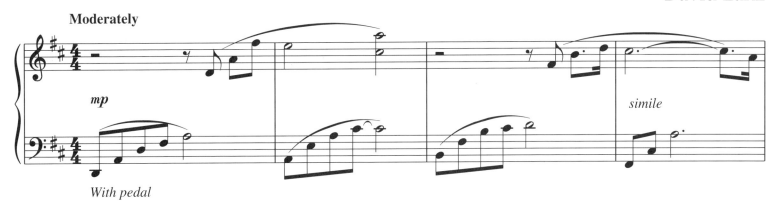

8vb _ loco

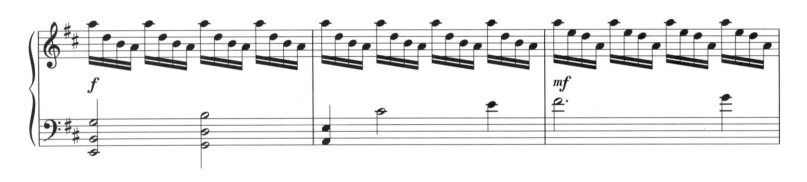

Nights in White Satin

Words and Music by
Justin Hayward
Arranged by David Lanz

A Whiter Shade of Pale

from "Straight to the Heart"

Words and Music by Keith Reid
and Gary Brooker
Arranged by David Lanz

Slowly, with feeling

With pedal

David Lanz

With over a dozen albums to his credit since his Narada debut in 1984, David Lanz has reached music lovers around the world with his extraordinary melodies, his tender romantic playing and the spiritual depth of his music.

Raised in Seattle, Lanz learned to play a number of different styles while still in high school including jazz, blues, rock and roll, pop and classical music. For many years, he worked in a variety of local clubs both as a band member and soloist. He has created a body of work which establishes the piano as one of the dominant voices in contemporary instrumental music.

Through all his accomplishments including a Gold record for CRISTOFORI'S DREAM in 1993, millions of records sold and critically acclaimed concert tours, Lanz has remained true to his inner vision of creating beautiful, profound music that invites each listener to a place of healing, rejuvenation and peace.

Discography

BELOVED
CHRISTMAS EVE
RETURN TO THE HEART
CRISTOFORI'S DREAM
SKYLINE FIREDANCE
HEARTSOUNDS
NIGHTFALL

With Paul Speer:
BRIDGE OF DREAMS
NATURAL STATES
DESERT VISION

With Michael Jones:
SOLSTICE

With Tingstad and Rumbel:
WOODLANDS

Songbooks

DAVID LANZ: CHRISTMAS EVE
THE DAVID LANZ COLLECTION
DAVID LANZ: BRIDGE OF DREAMS
DAVID LANZ: SOLOS FOR NEW AGE PIANO

Narada appreciates the support of its listeners, and we welcome your comments about the music of our artists. Narada publishes a free, semi-annual newsletter/catalog that features information about our artists as well as information on new recordings. You may receive future copies by writing us and joining our growing, worldwide family of quality-minded listeners. Please write to: Friends of Narada, 4650 North Port Washington Road, Milwaukee, WI 53212-1063 USA e-mail: friends@narada.com